Intermittent Fasting Meals: 50 Balanced Recipes

By: Kelly Johnson

Table of Contents

- Avocado and Egg Breakfast Bowl
- Grilled Chicken Salad with Olive Oil Vinaigrette
- Zucchini Noodles with Pesto and Grilled Shrimp
- Greek Yogurt Parfait with Berries and Chia Seeds
- Quinoa and Roasted Vegetable Bowl
- Salmon and Asparagus with Lemon Garlic Sauce
- Cauliflower Rice Stir-Fry with Tofu
- Turkey Lettuce Wraps with Avocado and Salsa
- Spinach and Mushroom Frittata
- Chickpea Salad with Cucumber, Tomato, and Feta
- Spicy Tuna Lettuce Wraps
- Grilled Chicken with Broccoli and Sweet Potato
- Baked Salmon with Avocado Mango Salsa
- Eggplant and Zucchini Lasagna
- Chia Seed Pudding with Almond Milk and Berries
- Chicken and Vegetable Stir-Fry with Almonds
- Baked Chicken Thighs with Brussels Sprouts
- Sweet Potato and Kale Salad
- Spaghetti Squash with Pesto and Chicken
- Grilled Shrimp with Quinoa and Roasted Veggies
- Cabbage Stir-Fry with Ground Turkey
- Cauliflower Crust Pizza with Veggies and Chicken
- Tuna Salad with Avocado and Arugula
- Sautéed Shrimp with Garlic and Spinach
- Grilled Steak with Roasted Vegetables
- Egg Salad with Mixed Greens
- Chicken and Avocado Lettuce Wraps
- Mushroom and Spinach Omelette
- Lemon and Herb Roasted Chicken with Cauliflower Rice
- Grilled Salmon with Spinach and Pine Nuts
- Turkey and Zucchini Meatballs with Marinara
- Green Smoothie with Spinach, Chia Seeds, and Almond Milk
- Shrimp and Avocado Salad with Lime Dressing
- Chicken and Broccoli Stir-Fry with Coconut Aminos
- Mediterranean Quinoa Salad with Olives and Feta

- Roasted Veggie Buddha Bowl with Tahini Dressing
- Grilled Chicken with Mango Salsa and Quinoa
- Cauliflower and Broccoli Soup
- Grilled Turkey Burgers with Avocado and Lettuce
- Cabbage and Carrot Slaw with Grilled Chicken
- Spaghetti Squash with Turkey Bolognese
- Grilled Shrimp with Kale and Roasted Pumpkin
- Baked Tofu with Veggies and Rice
- Greek Chicken Salad with Olives and Cucumbers
- Veggie and Black Bean Stir-Fry
- Avocado Chicken Salad with Mixed Greens
- Egg and Spinach Scramble with Tomatoes
- Grilled Steak Salad with Avocado and Lime Dressing
- Roasted Salmon with Mixed Greens and Lemon Dressing
- Lentil Salad with Roasted Vegetables and Lemon Vinaigrette

Avocado and Egg Breakfast Bowl

Ingredients:

- 1 ripe avocado, sliced
- 2 large eggs
- 1/4 cup cherry tomatoes, halved
- 1 tbsp olive oil
- Salt and pepper to taste
- Fresh cilantro or parsley for garnish (optional)

Instructions:

1. Heat olive oil in a skillet over medium heat. Crack eggs into the skillet and cook until the whites are set and yolks are still runny (or cooked to your liking).
2. In a bowl, arrange the sliced avocado, cooked eggs, and cherry tomatoes.
3. Season with salt and pepper, and garnish with fresh cilantro or parsley if desired.
4. Serve immediately for a hearty, nutritious breakfast.

Grilled Chicken Salad with Olive Oil Vinaigrette

Ingredients:

- 2 boneless, skinless chicken breasts
- 4 cups mixed greens
- 1/2 cucumber, sliced
- 1/4 red onion, thinly sliced
- 1/4 cup feta cheese, crumbled
- 1/4 cup cherry tomatoes, halved
- 1 tbsp olive oil (for grilling)
- **For the vinaigrette:**
    - 2 tbsp olive oil
    - 1 tbsp red wine vinegar
    - 1 tsp Dijon mustard
    - 1 tsp honey
    - Salt and pepper to taste

Instructions:

1. Preheat the grill to medium-high heat.
2. Brush the chicken breasts with olive oil and season with salt and pepper. Grill the chicken for 5-7 minutes per side, or until fully cooked.
3. While the chicken is grilling, whisk together the vinaigrette ingredients in a small bowl.
4. Slice the grilled chicken and arrange it on top of the mixed greens, cucumber, onion, tomatoes, and feta cheese.
5. Drizzle with the vinaigrette and toss to combine. Serve immediately.

Zucchini Noodles with Pesto and Grilled Shrimp

Ingredients:

- 2 medium zucchinis, spiralized into noodles
- 12-15 large shrimp, peeled and deveined
- 1 tbsp olive oil
- 1/2 cup pesto sauce (store-bought or homemade)
- 1 tbsp lemon juice
- 1/4 cup Parmesan cheese, grated
- Salt and pepper to taste

Instructions:

1. Heat olive oil in a grill pan or skillet over medium heat. Season shrimp with salt and pepper, and cook for 2-3 minutes per side until pink and cooked through.
2. In another skillet, sauté zucchini noodles for 2-3 minutes until tender, being careful not to overcook.
3. Toss the cooked zucchini noodles with pesto sauce until well coated.
4. Arrange the pesto zucchini noodles in a bowl, top with grilled shrimp, a drizzle of lemon juice, and sprinkle with Parmesan.
5. Serve immediately as a light and delicious meal.

Greek Yogurt Parfait with Berries and Chia Seeds

Ingredients:

- 1 cup plain Greek yogurt
- 1/2 cup mixed berries (blueberries, raspberries, strawberries)
- 1 tbsp chia seeds
- 1 tbsp honey (optional)
- 1/4 cup granola or nuts (optional)

Instructions:

1. In a bowl or glass, layer Greek yogurt, mixed berries, and chia seeds.
2. Drizzle with honey for sweetness, if desired.
3. Top with granola or nuts for a crunchy texture.
4. Serve immediately as a healthy breakfast or snack.

Quinoa and Roasted Vegetable Bowl

Ingredients:

- 1 cup quinoa, cooked
- 1 cup mixed vegetables (such as bell peppers, zucchini, and sweet potato), diced
- 1 tbsp olive oil
- Salt and pepper to taste
- 1/4 cup tahini sauce or dressing of choice
- Fresh herbs (optional)

Instructions:

1. Preheat the oven to 200°C (400°F).
2. Toss the diced vegetables with olive oil, salt, and pepper. Roast for 20-25 minutes until tender and slightly caramelized.
3. In a bowl, combine the cooked quinoa and roasted vegetables.
4. Drizzle with tahini sauce and garnish with fresh herbs if desired.
5. Serve immediately as a nourishing and filling meal.

Salmon and Asparagus with Lemon Garlic Sauce

Ingredients:

- 4 salmon fillets
- 1 bunch asparagus, trimmed
- 2 tbsp olive oil
- 3 cloves garlic, minced
- 1 lemon, juiced and zest
- Salt and pepper to taste

Instructions:

1. Preheat the oven to 200°C (400°F).
2. Place salmon fillets and asparagus on a baking sheet. Drizzle with olive oil and season with salt and pepper.
3. Roast for 12-15 minutes until the salmon is cooked through and flakes easily.
4. While the salmon and asparagus are roasting, sauté garlic in olive oil over medium heat until fragrant. Add lemon juice and zest, and stir to combine.
5. Drizzle the lemon garlic sauce over the roasted salmon and asparagus. Serve immediately.

Cauliflower Rice Stir-Fry with Tofu

Ingredients:

- 1 small cauliflower, grated into rice-sized pieces
- 200g firm tofu, cubed
- 2 tbsp olive oil
- 1/2 cup mixed vegetables (carrots, peas, corn, etc.)
- 2 tbsp soy sauce
- 1 tsp sesame oil
- 2 cloves garlic, minced
- 1/4 tsp ground ginger
- Salt and pepper to taste

Instructions:

1. In a pan, heat 1 tbsp olive oil over medium heat. Add tofu cubes and cook until golden and crispy on all sides, about 8 minutes. Set aside.
2. In the same pan, add the remaining olive oil and sauté garlic, mixed vegetables, and cauliflower rice for 4-5 minutes.
3. Add soy sauce, sesame oil, ground ginger, salt, and pepper. Stir well to combine.
4. Stir in the cooked tofu and cook for another 2 minutes.
5. Serve the cauliflower rice stir-fry hot as a low-carb meal.

Turkey Lettuce Wraps with Avocado and Salsa

Ingredients:

- 1 lb ground turkey
- 1 tbsp olive oil
- 1/2 onion, chopped
- 2 cloves garlic, minced
- 1 tbsp taco seasoning
- 8 large lettuce leaves (e.g., butter lettuce)
- 1 avocado, sliced
- 1/2 cup salsa
- Salt and pepper to taste

Instructions:

1. Heat olive oil in a pan over medium heat. Add the onion and garlic, cooking until soft.
2. Add ground turkey to the pan and cook until browned, breaking it up with a spoon.
3. Stir in taco seasoning, salt, and pepper, and cook for another 2 minutes.
4. Spoon the turkey mixture into lettuce leaves and top with avocado slices and salsa.
5. Serve immediately as a light and healthy meal.

Spinach and Mushroom Frittata

Ingredients:

- 6 large eggs
- 1 cup fresh spinach, chopped
- 1/2 cup mushrooms, sliced
- 1/4 cup shredded cheese (cheddar, feta, or your choice)
- 2 tbsp olive oil
- 1/4 tsp garlic powder
- Salt and pepper to taste

Instructions:

1. Preheat the oven to 180°C (350°F).
2. Heat olive oil in an oven-safe skillet over medium heat. Sauté mushrooms for 3-4 minutes until softened.
3. Add spinach to the skillet and cook for another 2 minutes, until wilted.
4. In a bowl, whisk eggs, garlic powder, salt, and pepper. Pour the egg mixture into the skillet and cook for 2-3 minutes.
5. Sprinkle cheese over the top, then transfer the skillet to the oven.
6. Bake for 10-12 minutes, or until the eggs are set and lightly browned on top.
7. Serve warm, cut into slices.

Chickpea Salad with Cucumber, Tomato, and Feta

Ingredients:

- 1 can (400g) chickpeas, drained and rinsed
- 1 cucumber, diced
- 1 cup cherry tomatoes, halved
- 1/4 cup red onion, thinly sliced
- 1/4 cup feta cheese, crumbled
- 2 tbsp olive oil
- 1 tbsp lemon juice
- Salt and pepper to taste
- 1 tbsp fresh parsley, chopped (optional)

Instructions:

1. In a large bowl, combine chickpeas, cucumber, tomatoes, red onion, and feta cheese.
2. Drizzle with olive oil and lemon juice, then toss gently to combine.
3. Season with salt, pepper, and fresh parsley, if using.
4. Serve immediately as a refreshing salad or refrigerate for 30 minutes before serving.

Spicy Tuna Lettuce Wraps

Ingredients:

- 1 can (160g) tuna, drained
- 1/4 cup mayonnaise
- 1 tbsp sriracha sauce (adjust to taste)
- 1 tsp soy sauce
- 1 tbsp green onion, chopped
- 1 tsp sesame oil
- 1/4 tsp garlic powder
- 6 large lettuce leaves (such as butter or romaine lettuce)

Instructions:

1. In a bowl, combine tuna, mayonnaise, sriracha, soy sauce, sesame oil, green onion, and garlic powder.
2. Mix well until the tuna is evenly coated.
3. Spoon the spicy tuna mixture onto lettuce leaves.
4. Serve immediately as a healthy and spicy snack or meal.

Grilled Chicken with Broccoli and Sweet Potato

Ingredients:

- 4 chicken breasts
- 2 sweet potatoes, peeled and cubed
- 1 bunch broccoli, cut into florets
- 2 tbsp olive oil
- 1 tsp garlic powder
- 1 tsp paprika
- Salt and pepper to taste

Instructions:

1. Preheat the grill to medium-high heat.
2. Toss chicken breasts in 1 tbsp olive oil, garlic powder, paprika, salt, and pepper.
3. Grill chicken for 6-7 minutes per side, or until cooked through.
4. While the chicken is grilling, toss sweet potato cubes and broccoli with 1 tbsp olive oil, salt, and pepper.
5. Roast sweet potatoes at 200°C (400°F) for 25-30 minutes until tender. Add broccoli to the same tray and roast for an additional 10 minutes.
6. Serve the grilled chicken alongside the roasted sweet potatoes and broccoli.

Baked Salmon with Avocado Mango Salsa

Ingredients:

- 4 salmon fillets
- 2 avocados, diced
- 1 mango, diced
- 1/2 red onion, finely chopped
- 1 tbsp cilantro, chopped
- 1 tbsp lime juice
- Salt and pepper to taste
- 1 tbsp olive oil

Instructions:

1. Preheat the oven to 180°C (350°F).
2. Drizzle salmon fillets with olive oil, salt, and pepper, then place on a baking sheet. Bake for 12-15 minutes until salmon is cooked through and flakes easily.
3. In a bowl, combine diced avocado, mango, red onion, cilantro, lime juice, salt, and pepper.
4. Top each salmon fillet with the avocado mango salsa and serve immediately.

Eggplant and Zucchini Lasagna

Ingredients:

- 2 medium eggplants, sliced thinly
- 2 zucchinis, sliced thinly
- 1 jar (24oz) marinara sauce
- 1 1/2 cups ricotta cheese
- 1 cup shredded mozzarella cheese
- 1/4 cup grated Parmesan cheese
- 1 egg
- 1 tsp dried oregano
- Salt and pepper to taste

Instructions:

1. Preheat the oven to 180°C (350°F).
2. Arrange eggplant and zucchini slices on a baking sheet, season with salt, and bake for 10-15 minutes until softened.
3. In a bowl, combine ricotta cheese, egg, oregano, salt, and pepper.
4. In a baking dish, layer marinara sauce, eggplant, zucchini, ricotta mixture, and mozzarella. Repeat layers until all ingredients are used.
5. Top with Parmesan cheese and bake for 25-30 minutes until the top is golden and bubbly.
6. Let cool slightly before slicing and serving.

Chia Seed Pudding with Almond Milk and Berries

Ingredients:

- 1/4 cup chia seeds
- 1 cup almond milk (or milk of choice)
- 1 tbsp maple syrup (optional)
- 1/2 tsp vanilla extract
- 1/2 cup mixed berries (blueberries, raspberries, strawberries)

Instructions:

1. In a bowl, combine chia seeds, almond milk, maple syrup, and vanilla extract. Stir well.
2. Cover and refrigerate for at least 4 hours, or overnight, to allow the chia seeds to absorb the liquid and thicken.
3. Top with fresh berries before serving.

Chicken and Vegetable Stir-Fry with Almonds

Ingredients:

- 2 chicken breasts, sliced thinly
- 1/2 cup almonds, slivered or chopped
- 1 red bell pepper, sliced
- 1 carrot, julienned
- 1/2 broccoli crown, cut into florets
- 2 tbsp soy sauce
- 1 tbsp sesame oil
- 1 tbsp olive oil
- 1 tsp garlic, minced
- Salt and pepper to taste

Instructions:

1. Heat olive oil and sesame oil in a large skillet or wok over medium heat. Add chicken and cook until browned and cooked through.
2. Add garlic, bell pepper, carrot, and broccoli to the pan. Stir-fry for 5-7 minutes until the vegetables are tender.
3. Stir in soy sauce, almonds, salt, and pepper.
4. Serve immediately, garnished with additional almonds if desired.

Baked Chicken Thighs with Brussels Sprouts

Ingredients:

- 4 bone-in, skinless chicken thighs
- 2 cups Brussels sprouts, halved
- 2 tbsp olive oil
- 1 tsp garlic powder
- 1 tsp paprika
- Salt and pepper to taste

Instructions:

1. Preheat the oven to 200°C (400°F).
2. Toss Brussels sprouts with 1 tbsp olive oil, salt, and pepper. Spread them on a baking sheet.
3. Rub chicken thighs with garlic powder, paprika, olive oil, salt, and pepper. Place them on the baking sheet with the Brussels sprouts.
4. Bake for 30-35 minutes until the chicken is fully cooked and the Brussels sprouts are crispy and tender.
5. Serve the chicken thighs with the roasted Brussels sprouts.

Sweet Potato and Kale Salad

Ingredients:

- 2 medium sweet potatoes, cubed
- 4 cups kale, chopped
- 1/4 cup olive oil
- 1 tbsp balsamic vinegar
- 1 tbsp honey
- Salt and pepper to taste
- 1/4 cup walnuts, toasted (optional)

Instructions:

1. Preheat the oven to 200°C (400°F).
2. Toss sweet potato cubes with 1 tbsp olive oil, salt, and pepper. Roast for 20-25 minutes until tender and lightly browned.
3. While the sweet potatoes roast, massage the kale with 1 tbsp olive oil until softened.
4. In a small bowl, whisk together balsamic vinegar, honey, salt, and pepper.
5. Toss the roasted sweet potatoes with kale and drizzle the dressing over the top.
6. Garnish with toasted walnuts if desired and serve.

Spaghetti Squash with Pesto and Chicken

Ingredients:

- 1 medium spaghetti squash
- 2 chicken breasts, grilled and sliced
- 1/2 cup pesto sauce (store-bought or homemade)
- 1 tbsp olive oil
- Salt and pepper to taste
- Fresh Parmesan cheese, grated (optional)

Instructions:

1. Preheat the oven to 200°C (400°F).
2. Slice the spaghetti squash in half lengthwise and remove the seeds. Drizzle with olive oil and season with salt and pepper.
3. Roast the squash halves cut side down for 35-40 minutes until tender.
4. Use a fork to scrape out the squash strands.
5. Toss the spaghetti squash strands with pesto sauce and top with grilled chicken slices.
6. Garnish with fresh Parmesan and serve warm.

Grilled Shrimp with Quinoa and Roasted Veggies

Ingredients:

- 1 lb large shrimp, peeled and deveined
- 1 cup quinoa, cooked
- 1 cup mixed vegetables (such as zucchini, bell peppers, and cherry tomatoes), diced
- 2 tbsp olive oil
- 1 tsp paprika
- 1 tsp garlic powder
- 1 tbsp lemon juice
- Salt and pepper to taste
- Fresh parsley for garnish

Instructions:

1. Preheat the grill to medium-high heat.
2. Toss shrimp with 1 tbsp olive oil, paprika, garlic powder, lemon juice, salt, and pepper.
3. Grill shrimp for 2-3 minutes per side until cooked through.
4. Toss diced vegetables with 1 tbsp olive oil, salt, and pepper. Roast at 200°C (400°F) for 20 minutes.
5. Serve grilled shrimp on a bed of quinoa with roasted vegetables and garnish with parsley.

Cabbage Stir-Fry with Ground Turkey

Ingredients:

- 1 lb ground turkey
- 1/2 head of cabbage, shredded
- 1 tbsp olive oil
- 2 cloves garlic, minced
- 2 tbsp soy sauce
- 1 tsp ginger, grated
- 1 tbsp rice vinegar
- Salt and pepper to taste

Instructions:

1. Heat olive oil in a large pan over medium heat. Add garlic and ground turkey, cooking until browned.
2. Add shredded cabbage, soy sauce, ginger, and rice vinegar to the pan. Stir-fry for 5-7 minutes until the cabbage is tender.
3. Season with salt and pepper, and serve immediately.

Cauliflower Crust Pizza with Veggies and Chicken

Ingredients:

- 1 medium cauliflower, grated into rice-sized pieces
- 1/2 cup mozzarella cheese, shredded
- 1/4 cup Parmesan cheese, grated
- 1 egg
- 1 tsp dried oregano
- 1/2 tsp garlic powder
- 1/2 cup marinara sauce
- 1 cup cooked chicken breast, shredded
- 1 cup mixed vegetables (such as bell peppers, mushrooms, and onions), sliced
- Fresh basil for garnish

Instructions:

1. Preheat the oven to 200°C (400°F).
2. Steam or microwave cauliflower rice for 5 minutes, then squeeze out excess moisture using a clean towel.
3. In a bowl, mix cauliflower rice, mozzarella, Parmesan, egg, oregano, garlic powder, salt, and pepper to form the crust.
4. Spread the mixture onto a baking sheet lined with parchment paper and bake for 15-20 minutes until golden.
5. Remove from the oven, spread marinara sauce, and top with shredded chicken and vegetables.
6. Bake for an additional 10 minutes, then garnish with fresh basil.

Tuna Salad with Avocado and Arugula

Ingredients:

- 1 can (160g) tuna, drained
- 1 ripe avocado, diced
- 2 cups arugula
- 1/4 cup red onion, finely chopped
- 1 tbsp olive oil
- 1 tbsp lemon juice
- Salt and pepper to taste

Instructions:

1. In a bowl, combine tuna, avocado, arugula, and red onion.
2. Drizzle with olive oil and lemon juice, then toss gently.
3. Season with salt and pepper, and serve as a light and healthy lunch or dinner.

Sautéed Shrimp with Garlic and Spinach

Ingredients:

- 1 lb shrimp, peeled and deveined
- 4 cups spinach, fresh
- 2 tbsp olive oil
- 3 cloves garlic, minced
- 1 tbsp lemon juice
- Salt and pepper to taste

Instructions:

1. Heat olive oil in a pan over medium heat. Add garlic and sauté for 1 minute.
2. Add shrimp and cook for 2-3 minutes per side until pink and cooked through.
3. Stir in fresh spinach and cook for another 2-3 minutes until wilted.
4. Drizzle with lemon juice, season with salt and pepper, and serve immediately.

Grilled Steak with Roasted Vegetables

Ingredients:

- 2 ribeye steaks
- 2 cups mixed vegetables (such as carrots, zucchini, and bell peppers), diced
- 2 tbsp olive oil
- 1 tsp garlic powder
- 1 tsp dried rosemary
- Salt and pepper to taste

Instructions:

1. Preheat the grill to medium-high heat.
2. Rub steaks with olive oil, garlic powder, rosemary, salt, and pepper. Grill steaks for 5-7 minutes per side for medium-rare (or longer to your preferred doneness).
3. Toss mixed vegetables with olive oil, salt, and pepper, and roast at 200°C (400°F) for 20-25 minutes, or until tender and lightly browned.
4. Serve the grilled steak with the roasted vegetables.

Egg Salad with Mixed Greens

Ingredients:

- 6 hard-boiled eggs, chopped
- 4 cups mixed greens
- 1/4 cup mayonnaise
- 1 tbsp mustard
- 1 tbsp lemon juice
- Salt and pepper to taste

Instructions:

1. In a bowl, combine chopped eggs, mayonnaise, mustard, lemon juice, salt, and pepper.
2. Toss with mixed greens and serve immediately as a light lunch or dinner.

Chicken and Avocado Lettuce Wraps

Ingredients:

- 2 chicken breasts, cooked and shredded
- 1 avocado, diced
- 1/4 cup red onion, chopped
- 1 tbsp lime juice
- 1 tbsp cilantro, chopped
- 8 large lettuce leaves (butter or romaine)
- Salt and pepper to taste

Instructions:

1. In a bowl, combine shredded chicken, avocado, red onion, lime juice, and cilantro.
2. Season with salt and pepper.
3. Spoon the chicken mixture into lettuce leaves and serve as a light and healthy wrap.

Mushroom and Spinach Omelette

Ingredients:

- 3 large eggs
- 1/2 cup fresh spinach, chopped
- 1/2 cup mushrooms, sliced
- 1 tbsp olive oil
- Salt and pepper to taste
- 1/4 cup shredded cheese (optional)

Instructions:

1. Heat olive oil in a skillet over medium heat. Add mushrooms and sauté for 4-5 minutes until soft.
2. Add spinach and cook for another 1-2 minutes until wilted.
3. In a bowl, whisk eggs with salt and pepper.
4. Pour the eggs into the skillet, swirling to evenly distribute. Cook for 2-3 minutes until the edges begin to set.
5. Flip the omelette, cook for another 1-2 minutes, then fold and serve. Optionally, sprinkle with cheese before folding.

Lemon and Herb Roasted Chicken with Cauliflower Rice

Ingredients:

- 4 chicken thighs, bone-in, skin-on
- 2 tbsp olive oil
- 1 lemon, juiced and zest
- 1 tsp dried thyme
- 1 tsp rosemary
- Salt and pepper to taste
- 1 medium cauliflower, grated into rice-sized pieces
- 1 tbsp butter
- 1 garlic clove, minced
- 1/4 cup fresh parsley, chopped

Instructions:

1. Preheat the oven to 200°C (400°F).
2. Rub chicken thighs with olive oil, lemon juice, zest, thyme, rosemary, salt, and pepper. Place on a baking sheet.
3. Roast chicken for 35-40 minutes, or until cooked through and crispy on the outside.
4. While the chicken cooks, heat butter in a pan over medium heat. Add garlic and sauté for 1 minute.
5. Add grated cauliflower, salt, and pepper, and cook for 5-7 minutes until tender, stirring occasionally.
6. Serve the roasted chicken alongside the cauliflower rice, garnished with fresh parsley.

Grilled Salmon with Spinach and Pine Nuts

Ingredients:

- 4 salmon fillets
- 2 tbsp olive oil
- 1 tbsp lemon juice
- 2 cups fresh spinach
- 1/4 cup pine nuts, toasted
- Salt and pepper to taste

Instructions:

1. Preheat the grill to medium-high heat. Brush salmon fillets with olive oil, lemon juice, salt, and pepper.
2. Grill salmon for 4-5 minutes per side, or until cooked through and flaky.
3. In a skillet, sauté spinach for 2-3 minutes until wilted.
4. Plate the grilled salmon and top with sautéed spinach and toasted pine nuts. Serve immediately.

Turkey and Zucchini Meatballs with Marinara

Ingredients:

- 1 lb ground turkey
- 1 zucchini, grated
- 1/4 cup breadcrumbs
- 1 egg
- 1/2 tsp garlic powder
- 1/2 tsp onion powder
- 1/4 cup Parmesan cheese, grated
- 1 cup marinara sauce
- Salt and pepper to taste

Instructions:

1. Preheat the oven to 180°C (350°F).
2. In a bowl, combine ground turkey, grated zucchini, breadcrumbs, egg, garlic powder, onion powder, Parmesan, salt, and pepper.
3. Form into meatballs and place on a baking sheet. Bake for 20-25 minutes, or until golden and cooked through.
4. Heat marinara sauce in a pan and simmer the meatballs in the sauce for 5 minutes.
5. Serve with a side of vegetables or over zucchini noodles for a low-carb option.

Green Smoothie with Spinach, Chia Seeds, and Almond Milk

Ingredients:

- 1 cup almond milk
- 1 handful fresh spinach
- 1 tbsp chia seeds
- 1 banana, frozen
- 1/2 cup pineapple chunks (fresh or frozen)
- 1 tbsp honey or maple syrup (optional)

Instructions:

1. In a blender, combine almond milk, spinach, chia seeds, banana, pineapple, and honey (if using).
2. Blend until smooth and creamy.
3. Pour into a glass and serve immediately for a refreshing, nutritious start to your day.

Shrimp and Avocado Salad with Lime Dressing

Ingredients:

- 1 lb shrimp, peeled and deveined
- 1 avocado, diced
- 2 cups mixed greens
- 1/2 cucumber, sliced
- 1/4 red onion, thinly sliced
- 2 tbsp olive oil
- 1 tbsp lime juice
- 1 tbsp fresh cilantro, chopped
- Salt and pepper to taste

Instructions:

1. Heat olive oil in a skillet over medium heat. Cook shrimp for 2-3 minutes per side until pink and cooked through.
2. In a large bowl, combine mixed greens, avocado, cucumber, red onion, and cooked shrimp.
3. Whisk together lime juice, olive oil, cilantro, salt, and pepper in a small bowl.
4. Drizzle the dressing over the salad and toss gently to combine. Serve immediately.

Chicken and Broccoli Stir-Fry with Coconut Aminos

Ingredients:

- 2 chicken breasts, thinly sliced
- 2 cups broccoli florets
- 1 tbsp olive oil
- 2 tbsp coconut aminos
- 2 cloves garlic, minced
- 1 tbsp ginger, grated
- 1 tbsp sesame seeds (optional)
- Salt and pepper to taste

Instructions:

1. Heat olive oil in a pan over medium heat. Add chicken and cook for 5-7 minutes until browned and cooked through.
2. Add garlic, ginger, and broccoli to the pan, stir-fry for 3-4 minutes.
3. Drizzle with coconut aminos and cook for another 2-3 minutes until broccoli is tender.
4. Serve with sesame seeds and enjoy a quick and healthy meal.

Mediterranean Quinoa Salad with Olives and Feta

Ingredients:

- 1 cup quinoa, cooked and cooled
- 1/4 cup Kalamata olives, sliced
- 1/4 cup feta cheese, crumbled
- 1/2 cucumber, diced
- 1/4 red onion, chopped
- 1/4 cup cherry tomatoes, halved
- 2 tbsp olive oil
- 1 tbsp lemon juice
- 1 tsp dried oregano
- Salt and pepper to taste

Instructions:

1. In a large bowl, combine cooked quinoa, olives, feta, cucumber, onion, and tomatoes.
2. Whisk together olive oil, lemon juice, oregano, salt, and pepper.
3. Drizzle the dressing over the salad and toss to combine.
4. Serve as a refreshing and light lunch or side dish.

Roasted Veggie Buddha Bowl with Tahini Dressing

Ingredients:

- 1 cup cooked quinoa
- 1 cup roasted vegetables (sweet potato, cauliflower, bell peppers, etc.)
- 1/4 cup tahini
- 1 tbsp lemon juice
- 1 tbsp olive oil
- 1 tbsp maple syrup
- Salt and pepper to taste
- Fresh cilantro or parsley for garnish

Instructions:

1. Roast vegetables at 200°C (400°F) for 25-30 minutes until tender.
2. In a small bowl, whisk together tahini, lemon juice, olive oil, maple syrup, salt, and pepper.
3. Assemble the Buddha bowl by placing quinoa at the base, topped with roasted vegetables.
4. Drizzle with tahini dressing and garnish with fresh cilantro or parsley. Serve immediately.

Grilled Chicken with Mango Salsa and Quinoa

Ingredients:

- 4 boneless, skinless chicken breasts
- 1 cup quinoa, cooked
- 1 ripe mango, diced
- 1/2 red onion, finely chopped
- 1/4 cup cilantro, chopped
- 1 tbsp lime juice
- 2 tbsp olive oil
- Salt and pepper to taste

Instructions:

1. Preheat the grill to medium-high heat.
2. Season the chicken breasts with olive oil, salt, and pepper. Grill for 6-7 minutes per side until fully cooked.
3. In a bowl, combine mango, red onion, cilantro, and lime juice to make the salsa.
4. Serve the grilled chicken on a bed of quinoa, topped with the mango salsa.

Cauliflower and Broccoli Soup

Ingredients:

- 1 head cauliflower, chopped
- 1 head broccoli, chopped
- 1 onion, chopped
- 3 cloves garlic, minced
- 4 cups vegetable broth
- 1 cup coconut milk
- 2 tbsp olive oil
- Salt and pepper to taste
- Fresh parsley for garnish (optional)

Instructions:

1. In a large pot, heat olive oil over medium heat. Sauté onion and garlic until soft, about 5 minutes.
2. Add cauliflower and broccoli to the pot, sautéing for another 5 minutes.
3. Pour in vegetable broth and bring to a boil. Reduce heat and simmer for 20 minutes, or until the vegetables are tender.
4. Blend the soup with an immersion blender until smooth. Stir in coconut milk and season with salt and pepper.
5. Garnish with fresh parsley and serve warm.

Grilled Turkey Burgers with Avocado and Lettuce

Ingredients:

- 1 lb ground turkey
- 1/4 cup breadcrumbs
- 1 egg
- 1 tbsp Dijon mustard
- 1 tbsp fresh parsley, chopped
- 1 avocado, sliced
- 4 lettuce leaves (for wrapping)
- Salt and pepper to taste

Instructions:

1. Preheat the grill to medium-high heat.
2. In a bowl, combine ground turkey, breadcrumbs, egg, mustard, parsley, salt, and pepper. Mix until well combined.
3. Form the mixture into 4 burger patties.
4. Grill the turkey burgers for 5-6 minutes per side, until fully cooked.
5. Serve the burgers wrapped in lettuce leaves with sliced avocado on top.

Cabbage and Carrot Slaw with Grilled Chicken

Ingredients:

- 2 cups shredded cabbage
- 1 cup shredded carrots
- 1 tbsp apple cider vinegar
- 1 tbsp olive oil
- 1 tsp honey
- Salt and pepper to taste
- 2 grilled chicken breasts, sliced

Instructions:

1. In a bowl, mix shredded cabbage and carrots.
2. In a small bowl, whisk together apple cider vinegar, olive oil, honey, salt, and pepper to make the dressing.
3. Toss the cabbage and carrot mixture with the dressing.
4. Top the slaw with sliced grilled chicken. Serve chilled.

Spaghetti Squash with Turkey Bolognese

Ingredients:

- 1 medium spaghetti squash
- 1 lb ground turkey
- 1 can (400g) crushed tomatoes
- 1 onion, chopped
- 2 cloves garlic, minced
- 1 tbsp olive oil
- 1 tsp dried basil
- 1/2 tsp oregano
- Salt and pepper to taste

Instructions:

1. Preheat the oven to 200°C (400°F).
2. Cut the spaghetti squash in half and remove the seeds. Drizzle with olive oil, salt, and pepper, and roast for 30-35 minutes, cut side down, until tender.
3. While the squash is roasting, heat olive oil in a pan over medium heat. Add onion and garlic, sautéing until soft.
4. Add ground turkey and cook until browned. Stir in crushed tomatoes, basil, oregano, salt, and pepper. Simmer for 15-20 minutes.
5. Use a fork to scrape the roasted spaghetti squash into strands. Top with turkey bolognese sauce and serve.

Grilled Shrimp with Kale and Roasted Pumpkin

Ingredients:

- 1 lb shrimp, peeled and deveined
- 2 cups kale, chopped
- 2 cups pumpkin, cubed
- 1 tbsp olive oil
- 1 tsp garlic powder
- 1/2 tsp smoked paprika
- Salt and pepper to taste

Instructions:

1. Preheat the grill to medium-high heat.
2. Toss shrimp with olive oil, garlic powder, smoked paprika, salt, and pepper. Grill for 2-3 minutes per side until cooked through.
3. Preheat the oven to 200°C (400°F). Toss pumpkin cubes with olive oil, salt, and pepper, then roast for 20-25 minutes until tender.
4. In a bowl, combine grilled shrimp, roasted pumpkin, and chopped kale. Serve immediately.

Baked Tofu with Veggies and Rice

Ingredients:

- 1 block firm tofu, pressed and cubed
- 2 tbsp soy sauce
- 1 tbsp olive oil
- 1 tsp sesame oil
- 1 cup rice, cooked
- 1 cup mixed vegetables (such as bell peppers, broccoli, and carrots), chopped
- 1 tbsp sesame seeds (optional)
- Salt and pepper to taste

Instructions:

1. Preheat the oven to 200°C (400°F).
2. Toss tofu cubes with soy sauce, olive oil, sesame oil, salt, and pepper. Spread on a baking sheet and bake for 20-25 minutes, flipping halfway through.
3. While the tofu bakes, sauté mixed vegetables in a pan with a little olive oil until tender.
4. Serve the baked tofu with sautéed veggies and cooked rice, garnished with sesame seeds if desired.

Greek Chicken Salad with Olives and Cucumbers

Ingredients:

- 2 chicken breasts, grilled and sliced
- 1 cucumber, diced
- 1/4 red onion, thinly sliced
- 1/4 cup Kalamata olives, sliced
- 1/4 cup feta cheese, crumbled
- 2 cups mixed greens
- 1 tbsp olive oil
- 1 tbsp lemon juice
- Salt and pepper to taste

Instructions:

1. Grill the chicken breasts and slice them into strips.
2. In a large bowl, combine the cucumber, red onion, olives, feta cheese, and mixed greens.
3. Drizzle with olive oil and lemon juice, and season with salt and pepper.
4. Top the salad with the grilled chicken and serve immediately.

Veggie and Black Bean Stir-Fry

Ingredients:

- 1 can (400g) black beans, drained and rinsed
- 1 red bell pepper, sliced
- 1 zucchini, sliced
- 1 carrot, julienned
- 1/2 cup corn kernels
- 2 tbsp olive oil
- 2 tbsp soy sauce
- 1 tsp garlic powder
- 1 tsp cumin
- Salt and pepper to taste

Instructions:

1. Heat olive oil in a large pan over medium heat. Add the red bell pepper, zucchini, and carrot, and sauté for 5-7 minutes until tender.
2. Stir in black beans, corn, soy sauce, garlic powder, cumin, salt, and pepper.
3. Cook for another 3-4 minutes, until heated through.
4. Serve immediately, either on its own or over rice.

Avocado Chicken Salad with Mixed Greens

Ingredients:

- 2 cooked chicken breasts, shredded
- 1 ripe avocado, diced
- 2 cups mixed greens
- 1/4 red onion, chopped
- 1/2 cup cherry tomatoes, halved
- 2 tbsp olive oil
- 1 tbsp lime juice
- Salt and pepper to taste

Instructions:

1. In a large bowl, combine shredded chicken, diced avocado, mixed greens, red onion, and cherry tomatoes.
2. Drizzle with olive oil and lime juice, and season with salt and pepper.
3. Toss gently and serve as a refreshing, light meal.

Egg and Spinach Scramble with Tomatoes

Ingredients:

- 4 large eggs
- 1 cup fresh spinach, chopped
- 1/2 cup cherry tomatoes, halved
- 1 tbsp olive oil
- Salt and pepper to taste

Instructions:

1. Heat olive oil in a pan over medium heat. Add the spinach and sauté for 1-2 minutes until wilted.
2. Add the cherry tomatoes and cook for another minute.
3. Crack eggs into the pan, and scramble with the veggies.
4. Cook for 3-4 minutes, until the eggs are fully scrambled.
5. Season with salt and pepper, then serve warm.

Grilled Steak Salad with Avocado and Lime Dressing

Ingredients:

- 2 ribeye steaks
- 1 avocado, sliced
- 4 cups mixed greens
- 1/4 red onion, thinly sliced
- 1 tbsp olive oil
- 1 tbsp lime juice
- Salt and pepper to taste

Instructions:

1. Preheat the grill to medium-high heat. Season the steaks with olive oil, salt, and pepper. Grill the steaks for 4-6 minutes per side, or to your preferred doneness.
2. While the steak rests, combine mixed greens, avocado, and red onion in a large bowl.
3. In a small bowl, whisk together olive oil, lime juice, salt, and pepper for the dressing.
4. Slice the grilled steak and add it to the salad. Drizzle with the lime dressing and serve immediately.

Roasted Salmon with Mixed Greens and Lemon Dressing

Ingredients:

- 4 salmon fillets
- 4 cups mixed greens
- 1 lemon, juiced and zest
- 2 tbsp olive oil
- Salt and pepper to taste
- 1 tbsp fresh dill, chopped (optional)

Instructions:

1. Preheat the oven to 180°C (350°F).
2. Season salmon fillets with olive oil, salt, pepper, and lemon zest. Roast for 15-20 minutes, or until the salmon is cooked through and flakes easily.
3. While the salmon roasts, prepare the salad by tossing mixed greens with lemon juice, olive oil, salt, and pepper.
4. Serve the roasted salmon on top of the salad, garnished with fresh dill, and enjoy!

Lentil Salad with Roasted Vegetables and Lemon Vinaigrette

Ingredients:

- 1 cup cooked lentils
- 1 cup roasted vegetables (such as sweet potatoes, bell peppers, and zucchini)
- 2 tbsp olive oil
- 1 tbsp lemon juice
- 1 tsp Dijon mustard
- Salt and pepper to taste
- 1/4 cup fresh parsley, chopped

Instructions:

1. Roast vegetables at 200°C (400°F) for 20-25 minutes until tender.
2. In a bowl, combine cooked lentils, roasted vegetables, and fresh parsley.
3. In a separate bowl, whisk together olive oil, lemon juice, Dijon mustard, salt, and pepper for the vinaigrette.
4. Drizzle the vinaigrette over the salad, toss gently, and serve immediately as a nutritious meal or side dish.